Blackbird Has Spoken

Blackbird Has Spoken

Katharyn Elizabeth Sheldryck

VANTAGE PRESS
New York

FIRST EDITION

All rights reserved, including the right of
reproduction in whole or in part in any form.

Copyright © 1996 by Katharyn Elizabeth Sheldryck

Published by Vantage Press, Inc.
516 West 34th Street, New York, New York 10001

Manufactured in the United States of America
ISBN: 0-533-11588-4

0 9 8 7 6 5 4 3 2 1

For my sister, Alison Gabrielle Blake,
without whose helpful suggestions this book never
would have been published. With love.

Contents

The Development of Early English Music and Its Influence on the Continent of Europe in Modern Times	1
Early Christians	1
The Development of the Organ	3
Opera	6
Music in Renaissance England	8
The Flute	14
The Clarinet	17
Introduction of Pianoforte	17
The Origins of the Harp	18
The Beggar's Opera	24
The Savoyard Operas	29
The Revival of Interest in the Guitar	36
Xylophones	41
Jazz	45
The Secret of Music	50
Conclusion	53
References	55

The Development of Early English Music and Its Influence on the Continent of Europe in Modern Times

Early Christians

In Roman times music was played on the drums and flute to accompany acrobatics and other public demonstrations, but the early Christians, imprisoned by the Roman emperor Pliny, A.D. 23–79, sang hymns in prison, which were probably antiphonal psalms. Saint Paul exhorted the Ephesians and Colossians to use hymns, psalms, and spiritual verses (Eph. 5:19; Col. 3:16).

Sophronius Eustus Hieronymus (c. 347–420), who became Saint Jerome, was one of the founding fathers of the Western church and translated the Latin version of the Bible, known as the Vulgate. Saint Jerome maintained that it was unseemly for a maiden even to know what a flute or lyre was.

The Jewish religion always gave a large place to music expression. One of the oldest inhabited sites in Palestine, indeed perhaps the oldest in the world, is the city of Jericho. Jericho was the first city conquered by the Israelites under Joshua, and after a seven-day siege the walls of the city fell at the sound of the trumpet.*

Many Jews who had been displaced from England in 1290 settled on the European continent, where the Jewish people had formed colonies, particularly in Germany, since the fourth century B.C.

Orlando di Lasso (1532–94) was born as Roland de Lassus in the Belgian town of Mons in 1532 and grew up in the tradition, native to Flanders and the Netherlands, which had already existed for hundreds of years, of performing music in the polyphonic style, that of many voices with varied melodic lines. Roland spent the years of his youth in Italy, and it was here in the land of the Renaissance, in which the achievements of a bygone age were glorified, that his musical education was most influenced, and where he adopted the Italian version of his name.

In 1557 Di Lasso entered the court of Albrecht V, who was a passionate music lover. Besides writing music of a spiritual nature in the order of masses, motettes, hymns, and magnificats, which service was funded in part by the religious establishments, Orlando was enabled to compose music for the court of a more worldly nature, such as Italian madrigals and French and German songs.

King David was a keen musician and played the organ; the hurdy-gurdy was one of the earliest keyboard instruments, resembling a portable organ, not unlike the instrument described in the Bible. This was distinguished from the "chair" or "choir" organ, as it came to be known once it was installed in a church. However, once the Christian

---

*Jericho was rebuilt and after exile in Babylon was resettled by the Jewish community, which refurbished the spring water. Judea became a separate state from Palestine under Theodocius II in the 1st century B.C.

had spread across Europe, the churches permitted only Christians to worship in them, and the synagogues where the Jews were permitted to practice their religion, did not contain organs as such until the nineteenth century.

The Greek philosopher and mathematician, Pythagoras, who lived from about 572 until 500 B.C., and who was also familiar with Greek metaphysics, drew up laws that regulate geometrical figures and form the mathematical basis of musical tones.

Notre Dame Cathedral in Paris became a centre for musical development in France in the twelfth century, providing a beautiful natural setting for the sung works of Josquin-du-pres and composers from Flanders, such as Palastrina, in the sixteenth century, and Dufay, who wrote for the recorder.

The Development of the Organ

The organ had always featured prominently in Jewish music, and there are records of many fine examples of the instrument dating back to the tenth century in England, notably in Worcester Cathedral.

The Danish composer, **Buxtehude,** who was born in 1637 in that part of Schleswig-Holstein which used to belong to Denmark, Oldesoe, and which now belongs to Germany, played and composed on the organ in the city of Lübeck. It was to Lübeck that Johann Sebastian Bach, who died in 1685, the year of George Frederick Handel's birth, would walk to hear the great 'father of organ music' play, and gain inspiration for his own compositions.

The organ **Johann Sebastian Bach** (1685–1750) used to play and compose on had pedals that were too short to enable him to move his feet fast and easily from one pedal to the other. A hundred years later Beethoven wrote in a letter to Freundenberg: "If an organist is master of this instrument, I rank him amongst the finest of virtuosi."

Organ playing reached a high point in England during the nineteenth century, and services at St. Paul's Cathedral in London would be filled to overflowing by a congregation attracted by the musical programme.

The art of unaccompanied madrigal singing flourished in Italy during the period of the Renaissance, and Flemish musicians who had studied in Italy, in particular the style of bel canto singing, returned to Northern Europe and, as skilled craftsmen, made improvements on many instruments, including the existing organs. Cremona, Guernara, and Stradivari violins were made in Italy, which attracted musicians and craftsmen to the country. Antonio Stradivari of Cremona, who lived from 1644 until 1737, was a pupil of the violin maker, Nicolo Amati, and, together with his two sons, he produced over a thousand violins and violoncellos between 1666 and 1737.

In order to understand the relationship between religiosity and art in sixteenth- and seventeenth-century Europe, it is important to see this in the context of the social and political power struggle under which artists, musicians, and painters worked, and the influence that the leading families of the day maintained upon them.

The House of Hapsburg, which took over a system of government first established by **Charles the Bold** (1277), when his daughter married into the family, provided the wealth for many artistic ventures; **Franz Joseph Haydn** (1732–1809) was dependent upon his patrons, the Esterhazy family, for continuing financial and spiritual support of his work. Joseph Haydn was born into that area of the Austro-Hungarian Empire known as Croatia in 1734, and his brother, Michael Haydn, was born three years later in 1737.

Both brothers had great musical talents and died within three years of each other, Michael in 1806 in Salzburg and Joseph in 1809 in Vienna, but the works of Joseph Haydn achieved a greater musical stature than those of his younger brother.

The city of Bruges was crucial to the attainments of the artist; Hans Memlingen, who was Rhenish by birth, but active in Bruges right up to his death in 1294, as it was the leading commercial centre of northern Europe, as well as the chief depot for rare and costly substances, including dyes and pigments from all over the world.

It was vital for the artistic attainments of the cities of Flanders and Brabant, as well as for Florence, that they had a wide range of highly sophisticated industries and crafts, which processed costly materials, produced fine goods, and generally sustained a cultured existence unobtainable in the other northern European trade centers, such as Lübeck or in France outside Paris.

Philip II of Spain (1527–98), who sent the Spanish Armada to subdue Britain, maintained a vigilant campaign of suppression of Dutch unorthodoxy in his dominions in the Netherlands, and he enforced the prohibition of any individuality of expression within the churches, which meant that it was forbidden for the people of the Netherlands to sing hymns, the souter liedekens or psalter-songs, from their own hymnbook, which was published in 1540 in the city of Antwerp.

The French composer, **André Ernest Modeste Grétry** (1741–1813), who was born in Liège, would most probably not have achieved such high recognition had he not resided principally outside France, which included studying in Rome. Grétry's musical output has virtually been adopted by the Belgium authorities as one of their own.

The melodies contained in early plainsong chants and

other vocal music were complete in themselves, and it was not until the time of the influential figures of **Johann Sebastian Bach** and **George Frederick Handel** (1685–1759) that music was modulated into major and minor keys during the late Baroque period.

Pope John XXII forbade the use of secular melodies as harmonised settings of portions of the church mass as he believed that musical enjoyment should not detract from the seriousness of the religious service. The only English cardinal ever to hold office as pope, **Adrian IV (Nicholas Breakspear),** banished the entire Jewish community from the islands of Britain in the twelfth century.

Opera

Claudio Monteverdi (1527–1643), the greatest of Italian composers, turned to writing operas again after he had left his native town of Mantua, where he had not been successful, and after he had established himself in Venice, which was the centre of Italy's cultural activity. His last opera, *L'incoronazione di Poppea,* was first performed in the autumn of 1642 in il Teatro SS Giovanni e Paolo in Venice, and unlike his previous works in this medium, was intended to be performed on a large stage in a public opera house. *L'incoronazione di Poppea,* is also remarkable for the way in which it deals with a political theme, the subject matter of which is not based on mythology, but on an event that happened during the reign of the Roman emperor, Nero, who lived from A.D. 54–68. Nero ordered his mother and Octavia, his wife, to be murdered and married his beloved Poppea, who at the time was the wife of the man who was later to become Emperor Otho.

In the composer's final great work, Monteverdi made

use of all the skills at his disposal, and the form in which he drafted the scenes, incorporating the music and the action with a single idea, together with the Decapoform in a set piece, remained the dominating style for later Venctian operas.

Claudio Monteverdi's search for naturalness and beauty led him at first to compose music for voices alone, maintaining the polyphonic style of singing, without instrumental accompaniment. The *vespro della Beata Verginne*, which Sir John Eliot Gardiner has recorded in St. Mark's, Venice, is a fine example of the timeless impact of Monteverdi's music.

In Rome, **Giovanni Francesco Parisani**'s opera, *Diana Schernita*, with music by **Giancinto Cornacchioli,** was performed in the home of **Baron von Hohen Rechberg**. This was the first operatic performance that was sponsored by the Berberine family, and was also one of the first operas with comic scenes in which Galileo's newest invention, the telescope, was ridiculed.

The *Masikalischen Exequiem* by **Heinrich Schütz** (1585–1672) was a monument in music to his patron, **Count Heinrich von Reuß,** who cared for his subjects in an exemplary manner, sparing them to a large extent from the ravages of the Thirty Years War (1616–48). Most of Europe was involved in this war of religion between Roman Catholics and Protestants at the end of which the autonomy of the states of Germany was upheld and the Peace of Augsburg of 1555 was confirmed, which granted freedom of worship to the princes and free cities of Germany, extending its provisions to include Calvinism.

In 1629, Heinrich Schütz was in Venice where he wrote his *Symphoniae Sacrae,* which appeared in print in the same year, and he also met Claudio Monteverdi.

Benedetto Marcello, who lived in Venice from 1686

until 1739, compiled an eight-volume collection of musical settings of the fifty psalms of King David, as well as writing a cantata, also titled "The Four Seasons" and his brother, Alessandro, who lived from 1684 until 1750, did much to further the concerto form, particularly with his oboe concerto,* as well as composing sonatas and cantatas.

The youngest son of Johann Sebastian Bach, John Christian, who was born in 1735 in Leipzig where his father held the position of cantor at the church of St. Thomas, spent six years in Italy before settling in London and becoming music master to Queen Charlotte and director of music at the Italian Opera in the King's Theatre, Haymarket.

Music in Renaissance England

Henry the Eighth (1491–1547) was himself a keen amateur musician and collector of musical instruments. He may also have composed the air "Greensleeves," which dates from this time, as well as encouraging the arts of music and dancing at his court. Henry the Eighth's court Inventory reveals an overwhelming majority of woodwinds compared to any other type of instrument. He possessed over seventy flutes, more than seventy recorders, twenty-five crumhorns, twenty-five shawms, thirteen dulceuses, as well as bagpipes and a tabor pipe (Anthony Baines, *History of Wind Instruments* [London: Faber, 1962]).

Henry VIII encouraged learning and the acquisition of knowledge in his court, and his first wife, **Catherine of Aragon,** was a patron of the humanist movement, which

---

*This instrument was first introduced into England by John Stanesby in 1750.

was challenging the traditional and scholastic outlook, not just in intellectual, but in court circles around the turn of the fifteenth century. Catherine received a Renaissance education, on the initiative of her mother, Queen Isabel of Spain. Together with her sisters, Catherine and the young princesses were taught by the Italian poet, Antonio Geraldine, and his brother Alessandro. As well as acquiring courtly and housewifely accomplishments, the *infantas* also studied Roman orators and poets, the Latin church fathers and Christian poets. Catherine also learnt Latin, French, and later English. This love of learning she wished to bestow on her daughter, who was to become Queen Mary I, but whose short reign lasted only from 1553 until 1558, when she was succeeded by her half-sister, Elizabeth, daughter of Henry's union with Anne Boleyn.*

Anne Boleyn had been educated chiefly in France, at the court of Francis I, and possibly also in the household of Margaret of Austria. Anne was drawn to the more evangelical French humanism, and to the scholars Jacques Lefevre d'Etaples and Clement Marot. She possessed an illuminated manuscript of the Book of Ecclesiastes, with the text in French and a commentary in English, as well as a manuscript French Psalter. These books were read by Anne Boleyn, who was praised by Loys de Brun for her reading of Scripture and other good works in French, including the salutary epistles of St. Paul, "in which are contained the whole manner and rule of a good life."

Elizabeth I (1533–1603), Henry the Eighth's daughter by his second marriage to Anne Boleyn, reestablished the Church of England as we now know it. Created in 1524,

*Dowling, "Culture at the Court of Henry VIII," *History Today*, vol. 41, June 1993.

reversed by Mary I, it was restored by the Act of Supremacy and the Act of Uniformity (passed by Parliament in 1559). In 1552 the Book of Common Prayer was restored after having been suppressed by Elizabeth's half-sister, Mary I.* At the coronation ceremony of Elizabeth I, the service was read in English as well as in Latin. The coronation of Queen Elizabeth I on 17 November 1558 almost undoubtedly included music of both a sacred and a secular nature together with dancing, as Elizabeth herself was very fond of dancing, particularly a dance called "La Volta," which was said to have been brought by musicians from Italy.

Queen Elizabeth I of England furthered the Protestant cause, which had been established by her father, Henry VIII, when he broke with the church of Rome over his divorce suit. The pope refused to annul Henry's marriage to Catherine of Aragon, although she had previously been married to Henry's older brother.

Thomas Tallis (1510–85) was master of the composers of the Chapel Royal, at least from Queen Mary's reign onwards, and wrote his great choral work *Spem in alium* on a commission from the Duke of Norfolk. It was possibly performed on such an occasion in Arundel House, London. Tallis may have used this opportunity to expand on the theme of a text that referred to the meaning of hope, the absolution of sins, and the blessedness of humility, in order to make a point to Queen Elizabeth, who at the time was engaged upon a course of government that called for the suppression of the Roman Catholic elements within the Church of England.

*G. J. R. Parry notes in his book *A Protestant Vision* that William Harrison detected a form a Protestantism in England in 1550, which saw "Papacy" as Antichrist, in a way similar to the Reformation movement in Germany, and critiqued the role of Elizabeth I in this matter.

The work is a forty-voice motet for eight five-part choirs, and Tallis carefully and expertly blended polyphony, which is the style of composition used at the beginning and end of the piece, with the choirs singing in harmony, with the use of counterpoint for the different parts to stress the emphasis of the words in the text, which were albeit in Latin.

Henry Purcell (1659–95) was born in London into a musical family and followed the path which is still followed by many British musicians of the present day, by first becoming a boy chorister. Henry's family was connected with music for the royal court, and in 1669 he joined the choir of the Chapel Royal. He remained connected with royal music after his voice had broken, and in 1673 a warrant was issued to admit Henry Purcell "in the place of keeper, maker, mender, repayrer and tuner of the regalls, organs virginalls, flutes and recorders and all other kind of wind instruments whatsoever in ordinary, without fee, to his Majesty." This king was **Charles II** who came from Scotland in 1660 to succeed his father, Charles I, who had been executed in 1649 after the Civil War, which had lasted from 1642 until 1648 and was followed by a protectorate during which period Oliver Cromwell, the leader of the opposition to the king, effectively ruled England and Wales. As a Roman Catholic he discouraged the writing of new music for the "English" church!

John Dowland was one of six lutenists at the court of Charles I, after leaving Denmark where he had also been a court musician, and travelling widely through Europe. John Dowland visited Italy and brought back with him a thorough knowledge of Italian "bel canto" singing, which included the practice of allowing women to appear and sing on the stage. Much of the stringed music of the time was played on the thorboe, a similar instrument to the lute, but with a greatly extended neck permitting longer strings—perhaps a forerunner of the modern violoncello, and on the archlute, which was the most versatile of all instruments.

Purcell continued his musical tuition with **John Blow,** and learnt much about the practical side of music making, and in particular, its lack of financial remuneration. Henry already had some songs in print before his appointment as organist at Westminster Abbey in 1679. His career then diverged into that of performer and composer, church musician, court musician, and composer for the stage.* Purcell's opera, *Faerie Queen,* draws its inspiration from Edmund Spencer's allegorical epic poem, in which Gloriana, the faerie queen, signifies both the abstract concept of glory, and that of Queen Elizabeth in particular.

Purcell's opera *Dido and Aneas* is perhaps the most popular of Purcell's operas today.

Sir Benjamin Britten, who lived from 1913 until 1976, made use of this theme in his operatic work, *Gloriana,* and his festival cantata for soloists, choir and organ, *Rejoice in the Lamb,* shows a perception of the influence of Henry Purcell's *Serenade,* in which the same devices are used to tell the story, this time with a happy end. Sir Benjamin Britten's *A Ceremony of Carols* stands in a similar relation to Purcell's *Hymn to St. Cecilia,* for which occasion Purcell composed regularly on November 22 until 1694, when the work was published posthumously.

In 1677, Purcell succeeded **Matthew Locke** (born in Exeter in 1630) as composer for the king's violins. Purcell's well-known set of trio sonatas for violins and continuo date

---

*At the coronation of Charles II in Scotland in 1651, music was played by eighty bagpipes, which are still a symbol of national pride.

from this period and have retained their popularity to this day.*

At the time when Henry Purcell was composing, the influence of the Italian style of composition, which contained abundant embellishment and improvisation, particularly in the singing of operatic arias, was beginning to be apparent in England, and Purcell's work shows evidence of this while remaining with the traditional style of English music. Purcell's music was used by John Dryden** in *King Arthur,* and in 1695 Shakespeare's *Tempest* was set to music during the reign of William (of Orange) and Queen Mary, who died in 1695. Purcell wrote the funeral music for this event.

The influence of Purcell's music was also seen at the French court of Louis XIV in Paris, especially in the work of **Jean Baptiste Lully,** who was born in Florence in 1632 and died in Paris in 1687, and François Couperin, who greatly added to the music available to be played on the harpsichord.

An interesting development in synagogue music took place in late sixteenth-century Italy, where a number of Jewish musicians came to hold high favour amongst the Gentile community. **Salommone de' Rossi,** who was en-

---

*Purcell's *Indian Queen* also contains music of the highest order.
**The poet and playwright, John Dryden, who was born in 1634 and lived until 1700, incorporated the music of Henry Purcell into his semi-operas, which, although calling for musical talent among the actors, did not require them to sing the entire dialogue, thus using the music for special effect, as William Shakespeare himself (1564–1616) did with his songs such as "O, mistress mine," from *Twelfth Night* and "Hark, hark the Lark." The influence of the Italian "bel canto" led to the singing of the soprano parts by women's voices, and no longer exclusively by young boys as had hitherto been the case.

gaged at the court of Mantua, and lived from 1587 until 1628, not only published books of madrigals and canozyonets, but also set psalms in the contrapuntal style in four to eight voices in Hebrew, for use in the synagogues.

The Amati family of Cremona attracted musicians to Italy through the manufacture of violins by Stradivari and his two sons who between them produced over a thousand violins and violoncellos between 1666 and 1737.

The Flute

The Lord Chamberlain's records of the "King's Musick" records seven recorder players and seven flute players at the funeral of Queen Elizabeth in 1603. The distinction between these two instruments seems to be unique to England at this time, as in the rest of Europe the word *flute* continued to be used as a generic term, denoting both the recorder and the transverse flute.

On the continent the word *flute* was sometimes used specifically for the recorder—as in the "Flüte of Pretorius" of the year 1619, and the "flauto" of Ganassi from the year 1535. Thus a variety of names developed in order to distinguish clearly between the two instruments.

Johann Sebastian Bach wrote the *Trio Sonata in C Minor* for flute, violin, and basso continuo, which forms the nucleus of the *Musical Offering* BMV 1079, and which came into being in the spring of 1747 when Bach was received in Berlin by the young flute-playing Prussian **King Friedrich II**, who had asked Bach for a theme upon which he could improvise. The *C Minor Sonata* seems like the echo of a great period in time through whose polyphonic style one could discern the first indications of the modern "galant" style, which the Prussian king liked so well.

Bach wrote a group of three sonatas for flute and harpsichord, BWV 1030–32, which rank among his greatest works for wind instruments. However, the duo- and trio-sonatas for violin or flute with obligato harpsichord, which were supposedly composed in Cöthen around 1717 when Bach was music director and conductor of music in the court of **Prince Leopold von Cöthen,** pose a question of authorship for stylistic reasons. The instrumentalist must not only solve ticklish breathing problems, but must achieve the inner musical unity of the contrasting sequences of four stylised dance movements.

The youngest son of Johann Sebastian Bach, John Christian, who was born in 1735 in Leipzig where his father held the position of music director at the church of Saint Thomas, spent six years in Italy before settling in London and becoming music master to Queen Charlotte and director of music at the Italian Opera in the King's Theatre, Haymarket.

Franz Joseph Haydn also travelled frequently to London during the decade after his friend **Wolfgang Amadee Mozart**'s death in 1791, and on numerous occasions played and conducted for the Royal Family. The king of England, **George I,** had originally been Elector George Louis of the German state of Hanover and moved his court to England in 1712. King George continued to employ the composer and musician, **George Frederick Handel,** who had taken up permanent residence there in 1712. He lived until 1759.

Handel purchased his harpsichords from the London firm of Shudi and Broadwood, which also included amongst their clients such prestigious European figures as Frederick II, known also as Frederick the Great, in Potsdam, and the Austrian Empress **Maria Theresa.** The name "Shudi" was added to Broadwood when the son of the Scottish firm of that name married into the Swiss family of

Shudi. Franz Joseph Haydn (1712–86) himself owned the largest model of harpsichord, and while he was in London, and as well as writing his *London Symphonies 93–104,* composed numerous works for the newly established medium of chamber music, which included the harpsichord. This instrument had previously been used to provide figured bass, or basso continuo, which was accompaniment to music usually played on the violin or on the violoncello, or a combination with both of these instruments together.

Joseph Haydn is also said to have studied the oratorios of Frederick Handel (Christopher Hogwood, *Handel,* London: Thames and Hudson, 1984) before composing his own oratorio *The Creation.* When this work was performed in London, it was not greeted with the same degree of warmth that the public had reserved for "their Handel," even when translated into the English language. Handel's oratorios had been designed to inform his audience on matters of religion, while at the same time offering them musical entertainment.

As with J. C. Bach's musical output for the harpsichord, notably his *Sonata 1 in B-flat Major,* so also did Joseph Haydn's own harpsichord sonatas come to be performed on the new forte-piano.

Antonio Vivaldi, who was born in 1678 and is remembered now for the development of the "concerto form" as he wrote music for solo stringed and wind instruments with the orchestra, was known as "the red priest" as he took Holy orders in 1703.* "The Four Seasons" describes the changing scenes of life.

William Boyce, who was born in 1711, was appointed

---

*J. S. Bach made arrangements of sixteen of these concertos for stringed instruments.

composer to the royal court of King George I in 1732, and is famous for the memorable song "Hearts of Oak," and for his trio-sonatas as well as for a valuable collection of cathedral music, which was published in 1760, and for the song "Hark, Hark the Lark." Another popular air at this time was the English song "Summer is a commin' in, loudly sing cuckoo," which is best described as a "round" song—each separate part is repeated a few bars after the previous one (a similar effect is achieved by the French part-song, "Frère Jacques").

The Clarinet

Mozart scored clarinet parts within his orchestral compositions, as well as writing a clarinet *Concerto, in A Major,* after hearing the playing of the virtuoso clarinettist, Anton Stadler. This piece received an enthusiastic reception from the public in Prague, a city for which Mozart held a great affection and which he honoured with the symphony he titled the *Prague Symphony.*

Introduction of Pianoforte

The Italian musician and craftsman, **Buzio Clementi,** who lived from 1752 until 1832, designed and built pianos in London. Clementi's piano studies, which he composed for this new instrument, remain standard works for piano players to the modern day, and indeed, had a strong influence on **Carl Ludwig van Beethoven,** who died in 1827, in the composition of his sonatas for the piano.

A notable assistant to, and pupil of Buzio Clementi was the Irishman **John Field,** whose original compositions for the forte-piano (as this instrument was originally referred to, because of its facility of permitting the music to be played loudly and softly) included a set of eighteen "nocturnes," *Peter's Edition 491*. This set of nocturnes appeared prior to those composed by Frederick Chopin, and indeed, Franz Schubert's last piano *Trio, in B-flat Major, op. 148*, is written in a similar form and is titled "Nottorno."

Franz Schubert was born in Vienna in 1797 and died there in 1828. One year after Carl Ludwig van Beethoven, whom he had admired greatly, but whom he only met infrequently. In 1822 Schubert composed his "Wanderer" fantasia for piano, and his *Symphony 8*, which he never completed. The set of variations for piano duet, which he wrote in 1827 and dedicated to the dying Beethoven, were much appreciated by the great man.

Franz Schubert was also a lover of the sound of the clarinet, for which he wrote a trio, together with pianoforte and soprano voice, which is titled "The Shepherd on the Rock," and a septet, in which the sounds of wind instruments are combined with stringed instruments.

Franz Schubert's music was never wholly accepted by the Viennese public at large, although the pianist Alfred Brendel has done much to establish the reputation of this composer alongside Mozart and Beethoven himself.

The Origins of the Harp

At the beginning of the second millennium B.C. an innovation was made in Mesopotamia with the introduction of the harp, which initially may have simply been an adaptation of the playing position of the arched harp. The vertical harp was plucked by the fingers of both hands, whereas the horizontal harp was plucked with a plectrum, whilst the left hand deadened, or damped the strings that were not sounded.

The Egyptian harp was closely related to that of Mesopotamia, but was a smaller harp on which a foot was developed. There was also a small shoulder harp. The angular harp was also current in Egypt. In Greece the harp was angular and vertical, but it was always regarded as a foreign instrument, and this was true in Rome as well. The harp was introduced into China at the end of the fourth century A.D., but never really established itself there, and, curiously, the harp was one of the few Eastern instruments that was not introduced directly into medieval Europe.

Exactly how the harp arrived in Europe remains a source for speculation, although there is much to be said in favour of the theory that this instrument was disseminated from Ireland, since the Irish were extraordinarily ubiquitous as early as the sixth century A.D. The early Irish bishops were not attached to a particular diocese, as has been the tradition of the church but wandered incessantly. However, even if the Irish are credited with having brought the harp to Europe, the question is not settled as to whether or not this was done exclusively by them or if the harp was also introduced independently as a musical instrument via traders, with the Near and Middle East.

John Field, an infant prodigy, was born in Dublin in 1782, travelled widely giving performances on the pianoforte, and together with Clementi visited St. Petersburg in 1802. In 1804, Field settled in St. Petersburg as a piano teacher, returning to London in 1832.

The Russian composer, **Rimsky-Korsakov,** was professor of music at the Music Conservatory at St. Petersburg after taking piano lessons in 1859, and making arrangements of the operatic tunes of Mikhail Ivanovitsch Glinka, who was born in 1804 in the Russian province of Smolensk.

Besides writing operas, Rimsky-Korsakov extended the repertoire of the saxophone, and his orchestral suite, *Sherherazade,* is a musical portrayal of the *Tales of the Arabian Nights.*

This style of *cantabile,* or singing method of piano playing, was appreciated in particular by Wolfgang Amadee Mozart, who was born in Salzburg in 1756, and his later keyboard works were certainly composed with the new pianoforte in mind.

Carl Philip Emmanuel Bach, who was born in Leipzig in 1714, taught his younger brother, John Christian, music in Berlin (where he studied before travelling to Italy in 1754) and revised the technique of keyboard playing, so that instead of crossing the middle finger over the other fingers, as had hitherto been the practice, the thumb was now passed underneath the hand, which also had the effect of sustaining the melody.

Carl Czerny, who was born in 1791, the year of Mozart's death, studied under Beethoven and Clementi and himself taught Franz Liszt, and further encouraged the fingering practice introduced by C. P. E. Bach. **Carl Ludwig** gave public performances of his own piano sonatas, as well as works by Mozart, in an attempt to raise money for Mozart's widow, Constanze, after Mozart died penniless and was buried in a pauper's grave outside the city of Vienna.

Wolfgang Amadee Mozart had belonged, together with his friend and teacher, Franz Joseph Haydn, to the Freemason's Lodge "Zur Kröning der Hoffnung," which had been closed down in the year prior to Mozart's death by the Emperor Franz Joseph in an attempt to counteract subversive influences, which were believed to threaten the Hapsburg Empire. In France at the time of the French Revolution in 1789, Freemasonry was very widespread, and the French "Lodges" even admitted women, which was not the case in Austria. In an insecure financial position, and without help from his "Brothers," Mozart was forced to take on more commissions than he had strength to perform.

The Mozart Operas

In his opera *The Magic Flute,* Mozart reveals in his music and through the action, some of the secrets of the Freemason's Lodge, including instances of the triple knock on the door of the lodge, which was the sign a member would give to gain entry.

During Mozart's life-time, his most celebrated opera was *The Marriage of Figaro,* which was permitted to be performed only in the Italian language, due to the fact that the heroine, Suzanna, who is being courted by the hero, Figaro, is a chambermaid, and at the time of the Austro-Hungarian empire, such a match, which had not been arranged by the families concerned, would not have been considered suitable.

The marriage of the Austrian Emperor Leopold II, who did not directly oppose secret societies, as he was a Prosicritean himself, inspired Mozart to write this opera.

In the opera *Cosi fan Tutti,* which Mozart started writing in the autumn of 1789, the crucial distinction made during the period of the Enlightenment, between vows in church and contracts made under the law, is explored by Mozart as the basis of social cohesion in a society ruled by the aristocracy.

Mozart's opera, *The Abduction from the Serail,* which was written in 1782, and at once achieved great popularity, demonstrated Mozart's genius in operatic characterisation for the Viennese opera-going public. In this opera Mozart showed that he could write a successful musical drama in German, a venture in which Emperor Franz Joseph encouraged him, although he was quoted as saying that the music was almost too beautiful for their ears. He was also quoted as saying that there were too many notes—an allegation that was repudiated by Mozart. "There are no more notes than are necessary to the music" was his reply.

Mozart paid tribute to Joseph's enlightened methods of government by permitting the hero of the plot, Selim, to act in a magnanimous manner, and to grant the son of his enemy his life and to allow the Christians to return home.

Mozart developed the repertoire of the clarinet both in the orchestra and as a solo instrument. The clarinet concerto in A major was originally written for basset-horn and orchestra. Mozart, Weber and Spohr also wrote music for the instrument which was played in the Haymarket in 1751, and had a regular place in military bands from 1762. Richard Strauss seems to have had a special fondness for the instrument as nearly the entire family of the instrument makes an appearance in his music to the opera *Salome*.*
Joseph Haydn does not make so much use of the clarinet, which did not have a regular place in German orchestras until 1772, and when George Frederick Handel wrote *Messiah*, it was originally scored without clarinets, although the Huddersfield Symphony Orchestra does perform the work with a clarinet part, and to good effect.

Carl Ludwig van Beethoven was born in Bonn in 1770 and died in Vienna in 1827, aged fifty-six years, and more than any other composer deserves to be called "the Shakespeare" of music. Beethoven's music reaches to the heights

---

**London Review of Books,* July 1994.

and plumbs to the depths of the emotions of the human spirit, and indeed it was his own ambition to be called a "tone-poet."

The complete mastery of musical technique possessed by Beethoven enabled him to compose towards the end of his life the sublime string quartets, written when his faculties of sight and hearing were already failing, and thus Beethoven found a means of timeless expression of his emotions after suffering much pain.

When Beethoven was alive, music was seen as a recognised luxury of wealth and position (apart from the simplicities of popular music and the ritual of church music) and nearly every composer up to that time had been dependent upon the regular emoluments for musical service at some or one of the great courts of Europe, of which Germany had a number.

Ludwig was born into a poor but musical family in the service of the Elector of Cologne at Bonn, and his first teacher was his own father. Neefe was the chief musician of the court. The boy became his musical assistant in the capacity of orchestral harpsichordist, which involved the skills of conducting. He also received tuition on the violoncello, which he played in the Elector's orchestra which provided valuable insight* into the art of scoring music for the orchestra, and gave him a knowledge of the possibilities of the string section in particular, enabling him to compose his great *Violin Concerto in D Major, op. 61,* which dates from the year 1806.

When Beethoven was seventeen years of age, he was sent by his elector on a visit to Vienna, where he was

---

*Although he never visited Britain, he admired the people of the country and wrote five variations on "Rule Britannia" for pianoforte.

instructed by Mozart who fully recognised Beethoven's musical genius. In the absence of any organised system of public concerts and the scarcity of music printing—there were no copyright laws—Beethoven could not throw himself with confidence upon the sufferance of a wide public but remained dependent upon the support of that body of amateurs who had recognised his great ability as a pianist when he first came to Vienna, and later found this to be surpassed by his genius as a composer.

Beethoven was an ardent admirer of the works of George Friedrich Handel, which he recommended to his patron and later pupil, Count Rudolph. In a letter of the year 1819, and to Edward Schülz, who visited him in 1823, Beethoven is quoted as saying, "Handel is the greatest composer who has ever lived."

The Beggar's Opera

John Gay's work was overshadowed by the literary output of the Irish-Anglo writer **Jonathan Swift,** who was born in Ireland of English parentage in 1667 and died in England in 1745. He lived at a time when it was becoming possible for a prominent literary figure to discuss matters of a topical nature with members of the royal family, and his book *The Last Four Years of Queen Anne* deals with the reign that preceded the Hanovarian kings, and with problems caused by pamphleteering in particular. *The Beggar's Opera* appeared in 1728 and is a parody of such figures of the English establishment such as Alexander Pope, and the seriousness of Italian opera, high or low.

The musical arrangements of this opera were instigated by Dr. Pepusch, who used popular songs of the times, French airs, dance tunes from Scotland and snatches from the music of Purcell and Handel to depict a street life of the common people. The fashionable Italian opera of the period was thus derided, although George Frederick Handel based his own compositions on this style, while leaving much scope for the individual artists to improvise, particularly in the arias, according to their own temperament and ability.

The German musician of the inter-war period, Kurt Weill revived Gay's idea in the *Drei Groschen Oper,* which sets to music words by Berthold Brecht, depicting the decadent way of life that existed in Berlin, in the years following the end of the First World War. During this period much of Germany's failure to achieve status as a world power was blamed on "foreigners" and "outsiders."

Joseph Haydn is also said to have studied the oratorios of Frederick Handel (Christopher Hogwood, *Handel*), before composing his own oratorio *The Creation,* but when the work was performed in London it was not greeted with the same degree of warmth that the public had reserved for "their Handel," even when translated into the English language. Handel's oratorios had been designed to inform his audience on matters of religion, while at the same time offering them musical entertainment. In 1791 Haydn was made Doctor of Music in London.

George Frederick Handel's music was undoubtedly also indebted to the work of his predecessor at the English court, Henry Purcell, whose style itself may have owed much of its sophistication to the French composers d'Angelbert and Louis Couperin, who in 1693 became chief organist to the Sun King Louis XIV. However, his music always portrays a robustness and sonority that is peculiarly English, and Handel never visited Paris.

Handel wrote music specifically for court functions, music such as the *Water Music* and *Fireworks Music,* which were enthusiastically received by the public. On 27 March 1742, the first performance of *Messiah* was given in Dublin, at the request of the governor of this city, and the proceeds of the concert were used to improve conditions for the inmates of the local prisons. During his visit to Dublin, Handel also met Mrs. Cibber, an actress and the sister of the English composer **Thomas Arne,** who lived from 1710 until 1778, and who arranged musical settings for many English songs, such as "Where the Bee Sucks." Handel's own melody "Where'er You Walk" is a similar example of this kind.

Felix Mendelssohn-Bartholdy was born in 1809 in Hamburg, and his grandfather was the philosopher Moses Mendelssohn—the name Bartholdy was only added after the child had been baptised into the Christian faith. This necessary step was taken in order to enable Felix to pursue a musical career. Gustav Mahler, who lived from 1860 until 1911 would also have been unable as a Jew to obtain the position of conductor of the Vienna Opera House, had he not previously entered the Roman Catholic church.

Felix Mendelssohn-Bartholdy attained musical maturity with the composition of the overture to *A Midsummer Night's Dream,* drawing on William Shakespeare's play of the same name for inspiration, which he completed in 1826.

In 1829, when Mendelssohn toured Scotland, he was inspired by the sight of the caves and the rocks on the coast to compose the "Hebrides Overture," and the *Scottish Symphony*. He also composed the "Italian," honoring another country in which he loved to travel.

Mendelssohn conducted the Lower Rhine Festival at Düsseldorf in 1834 and again in 1835, when he also established the Leipzig Gewandthaus Orchestra. This orchestra, which was created out of the previous Bach Academy, was formed to perform the works of Johann Sebastian Bach, which had been neglected since his death in 1750. Thus J. S. Bach's great oratorium, the *St. Matthew Passion,* came to be performed again after the manuscripts had been assumed to be permanently mislaid.

While in Scotland, Felix Mendelssohn also wrote his orchestral suite *Fingal's Cave,* and his love of England led him to frequent the area outside London known as "Burnham Beeches" with such regularity, that one stretch of woodland is known as 'Mendelssohn's Walk,' where a seat has been placed beneath his favourite beech tree bearing a plaque in memory of this great composer.

Mendelssohn's *Symphony in D Minor, op. 107,* called the "Reformation" Symphony, has as its theme the tune of the Lutheran hymn "Ein Feste Burg ist unserer Gott," and so reiterating Luther's call to see the church as a haven of safety, rather than for seeking for power on earth.

Felix Mendelssohn's Oratorio *Elijah* was enthusiastically received by the British public when he conducted the performance in Birmingham in 1846. His skill as a musician generally was acknowledged by membership of the Royal Society of Music.

Mendelssohn's tenth visit to England in 1847 was also his last, for scarcely had he returned to Germany, when his sister, Fanny Hensel, herself a remarkable composer of music, died, and this final blow accelerated Felix Mendelssohn's decline into illness and depression. Felix died soon after his sister, leaving a wife and five children. Felix Mendelssohn's *Violin Concerto,* written in 1844, is characteristic of his great talents, which in many ways are reminiscent of the young Carl Ludwig van Beethoven.

The English composer and church musician, **Samuel Wesley,** befriended Mendelssohn during his visits to England, and also did much to promote an interest in the works of J. S. Bach, whose work had been largely neglected by the British public since his death.

In 1993, a manuscript was found in an organ loft in the city of Antwerp that contained a hitherto unknown mass composed by **Hector Berlioz** who lived from 1803 until 1869. His music had previously been considered as the musical expression of his literary ideas.

Robert Schumann (1810–56) was among the associates of the Leipzig Music, which opened in 1843. The violinist Ferdinand David, was also connected with the school. However, 150 years later, when Germany is a one-nation state, the Leipzig Gewandthaus Orchestra, which has been associated with great conductors such as Bruno Walter (who was forced to leave in 1933 on racial grounds) and Kurt Masur, who took office in 1954, has been little affected by trends of playing the music of early composers on original instruments.

During the nineteenth century, the work of **George Frederick Handel** was also surprisingly neglected in England, and indeed, fresh interest was only shown in *Messiah* after World War II, when performances were given in the Royal Festival Hall, London, in 1959, although Handel's opera *Julius Caesar* was performed in English in 1930. In 1933 Handel's opera *Rinaldo* was also performed in England, and 1939 a performance was given of *Rodelinda,* but it was in Handel's country of origin, namely in Germany, that the main body of his works was given a new lease of life. In 1920 the university town of Göttingen gave a performance of *Rodelinda,* the first time since 1754 that a German audience had seen a performance of an opera by "Händel."

During the war years, the "cleansing" of German art from Jewish influence accelerated in its intensity, and complete texts of Handel's oratorios were written anew. *Judas*

Maccabeaus was transformed by Klöcking and Hacke into *Wilhelm von Nassau,* and as a result of the success of this venture, the team was assigned the task of rewriting *Israel in Egypt* as *Mongulsturm,* scheduled for completion by the end of 1942.

Volkmar Braunbehrens asserts in his biography of Mozart's contemporary and rival, **Antonio Salieri,** who was closely associated with Mozart during the years 1784–86, the operas of Salieri and Mozart would have had less impact on their public had it not been for the work of the Jewish-Italian librettist **Lorenzo Da Ponte.**

The Savoyard Operas

These operas, which were produced in London from 1881 onwards by the D'oyle Carte Theatre Company, were written by **William Gilbert** and set to music by **Arthur Sullivan.** They are a series of comic operas which poke fun at the late Victorian way of life and include such favourites as *Trial by Jury,* from the year 1875, *The Pirates of Penzance,* written in 1880, *Iolanthe* (1882), and *The Gondoliers,* which dates from 1889.

Gilbert and Sullivan's last two operas, which they wrote after a serious quarrel, *Utopia Limited* (1893) and *The Grand Duke* from the year 1896, are scarcely ever performed these days—and a similar fate has befallen some of the less well-known plays of the great British playwright, William Shakespeare, such as *Titus Adronicus,* owing to problems of stage production.

Frederick Delius was born in Bradford in 1862 of German descent, and died in France in 1934, having spent the last forty-six years of his life in that country. The operas that Delius wrote were at first well-received in Germany, with *A Village Romeo and Juliet* being performed in Berlin in 1907, followed by a production of *Fennimore* in Frankfurt-on-Main in 1919, and a performance of 'Koanga' at Elberfeld took place in 1904. It was mainly due to the efforts of Sir Thomas Beecham, who organised a great Delius Festival in London in 1929, that the work of this composer became more widely known to British audiences, and one of his compositions, "On Hearing the Fist Cuckoo in Spring," is a tone poem representing the heart of Delius's response to nature's poetry, evoking the magic of the English countryside. It captures a sense of the yearly reawakening of the scene with the coming of spring, and a delightful passage on the clarinet clearly depicts the call of the cuckoo, a device also used by Gustav Mahler in his orchestral composition *Des Knabens' Wunderhorn*.

Richard Strauss was born in Munich in 1864, ten years before the British composer **Gustav Theodore von Holst**, who was born in Cheltenham in 1874. Richard Strauss became solo horn player in the Munich Opera, which gave him the orchestral experience to enable him to compose in particular music for wind instruments, including an oboe concerto. He also wrote settings for twenty-seven songs from *Des Knabens Wunderhorn* by Gustav Mahler, who had based his collection on the *Brentano Lieder,* which is the earliest known collection of German folk songs.

The *Four Last Songs* of Richard Strauss were composed in 1948, when Strauss was eighty-four years of age, and consist of musical settings of poems by Hermann Hesse and Joseph von Eichendorf. The first performance of the work took place in London at a concert given by the Philharmonia Orchestra with the Danish soprano, Kirsten Flagstad, after the composer's death in 1949.

The music seems to belong in the previous century, in the tradition of Brahms, Schumann and Schubert—who was a pupil of the Viennese master, Antonio Salieri. It has little in common with the music of the avantgarde, such as the Viennese-Jewish composer Arnold Schoenberg (1874–1951) or with the new rhythmic developments and juxtapositions of tonality employed by Igor Stravinsky, who was born in St. Petersburg on 1888, and died in New York in 1971 after a life-long service to the cause of Russian music, in particular with regard to the art of ballet, especially as portrayed in the West by the group led by Diagolev. Stravinsky's ballet *The Rites of Spring* may also be seen as relevant to the times when the dinosaurs roamed the earth, unimpeded by man's technology.

Gustav Holst, whose ancestors were originally from Scandinavia, decided to delete the title "von" from his name due to the anti-German sentiment that was prevalent in England after the outbreak of World War I. He spent five years studying music at the Royal College of Music from the age of nineteen, where he received lessons in composition from the Irish composer and musician, Charles Stanford.

After leaving the Royal College of Music, Holst joined an orchestra which played during the summer as a tuba player in order to earn some money but in 1906 he took direction of the music of St. Paul's Girls School in London, and gave exceptional importance to the singing of madrigals, especially the madrigals from Suffolk, and music by the old English composers, Morley (1543–1623), Byrd, and Thomas Tallis. During the First World War, Holst used his experience and love of music to organise musical activities among soldiers stationed in Salonica and Constantinople and became very popular with the men with whom he worked.

Holst shared his interest in English folk songs with **Ralph Vaughan Williams,** who was born in 1872, and died in 1958, and this inspired him to compose the *St. Paul's Suite for Strings,* which dates from 1913.

The most popular of Holst's compositions remains the "Planets" Suite, in which the composer creates a musical setting for each of the planets which are known through astrology. In the "Hymn of Jesus," a Gnostic tendency is portrayed through the music. The Huddersfield Choral Society gave the first performance of this work, and this Society also maintained a tradition of performing Handel's *Messiah* on a regular basis, and one version of a recording of the concert includes clarinets among the woodwind, although Handel did not require this in the original score.

Charles Stanford, the Irish composer and musician, was born in Dublin in 1852 and contributed much to the repertoire of British church music, besides a memorable clarinet sonata, containing an Irish lament. He was a professor at the Royal College of Music. He died in London in 1914.

Sir Arthur Bliss (1891–1975) was a pupil of Stanford, Holzt and Vaughan Williams at the Royal College of Music in London, and his Clarinet Sonata, which has an equally important piano part, dates from 1916, and uses all the tonal colour of the instrument to evoke more than just sound from the music, evoking meaning from words such as those written by the poet, Rupert Brooke, shortly before he died during the First World War. The opening lines: "If I should die, think only this of me: That there's a corner of some foreign field that is forever England . . . and in that dust a richer dust concealed."

Ralph Vaughan Williams also studied in Paris with **Maurice Ravel,** and worked with **Max Bruch** in Berlin; but the essential character of his music was unaffected by the European influence, although his "Concerto for Tuba and Orchestra" is reminiscent of the orchestration of Richard

Strauss. Vaughan Williams's later orchestral works bridge the period between original and new instrumentation, which is evident in the *Norfolk Symphony* in which the different tone-colours of the orchestra blend harmoniously together.

"The Lark Ascending" evokes the idyllic English countryside, with the lark depicted on the violin against the backdrop of the orchestra, and as a collector of folk songs, Vaughan Williams uses the tune of "Greensleeves" in his Falstaff opera, *Sir John in Love,* which he wrote in 1929. A theme by Thomas Tallis appears in his *Fantasia.*

The *Symphonia Antartica* by Vaughan Williams brings to mind another of nature's great wildernesses, and the choral effects produce almost the sound of the wind blowing through wide-open space.

Vaughan Williams's *Concerto for Piano, Strings and Mouth Organ* provides another opportunity for an instrument that is seldom heard in the concert hall to make its appearance on the stage. The French composer, Jean Francaix, has in a similar way given the accordion the solo part with an orchestra in a Concerto which he wrote for the instrument in 1992, recalling the sounds heard on the streets in the cafés of Paris, and all over France.

In 1928 it was the German composer **Paul Hindemith** (1895–1963) who brought to the attention of the British public at a Promenade Concert given in the Royal Albert Hall, the viola concerto of the British composer, **William Walton**. This composer later turned his attention to the writing of music for the film industry, and emerged as the supreme exponent of this art, with a flair for building up tension and atmosphere as in Shakespeare's *Henry V, Hamlet,* and *Richard III.* William Walton wrote a series of *Variations for Orchestra* on a section of the slow movement of Hindemith's *Cello Concerto* and was awarded a knighthood before he died in 1982. The music of Paul Hindemith brings alive the busy intensity of the industrial scene, with change being brought about by mechanisation and modern technological inventions.

Peter Iljitsch Tchaikowsky, who was born in 1840, visited Berlin in 1867 and became acquainted with the operatic style of the German composer **Richard Wagner**, who was born in Leipzig, and attended the Thomas Schule there. Tchaikowsky was impressed by the spectacle and sheer scale of Wagner's operatic style, but it was said that he found some of the music "boring." This was in contrast to the respect he had for the compositions of Johannes Brahms, with whom he became firm friends, although the style of Brahms' music was very different to his own. Tchaikowsky was never considered to be a member of the group of five Russian composers who had dedicated themselves to composing music of a nationalistic nature, as did **Rimsky-Korsakov** (1844–1908), **Balakirev, Glinka,** and **Mussorgsky,** whose composition *Pictures at an Exhibition,* written in 1874 for piano solo, has kept a firm place in the concert repertoire.

Tchaikowsky's music was inspired by the folk melodies of his country, as well as by the Russian ballet, which was founded in St. Petersburg by Tsar Peter the Great, who lived from 1686 until 1725, and who oriented himself in accordance with Western tendencies in the reforms he made to his kingdom. Tchaikowsky's *Nutcracker Suite,* op. 71, was based on the novel by A. Hoffmann, called *The Nutcracker and the Mouse King,* and Tchaikowsky wrote the libretto for the ballet as well. While Tchaikowsky was still working on the music for this ballet, he travelled to Paris in 1891 to conduct a concert of his own compositions. During this stay, he met Mustel, who so impressed him with his new-fangled instrument, the celeste, that Tchaikowsky used it in his ballet for the "Dance of the Sugar Plum Fairy."

The *1812 Overture,* which Tchaikowsky wrote in October 1880 in less than one week, is so called because of the sound of cannons being fired off, which occurs as the end of the work, which recalls the progress of Napoleon's armies across Europe, remains the most popular of all Tchaikowsky's compositions. However, at the time he wrote it, Tchaikowsky valued the piece as having little value, because he had written it "without warmth and love."

Another great Russian composer, **Sergie Rachmaninov,** who was born in 1873, wrote a *Piano Concert,* and a *Prelude in C-sharp Minor* which he performed all over Europe, including in England in 1899. The Russian Revolution of 1917 caused Rachmaninov to leave Russia, and he made his new home in the United States of America. Rachmaninov also wrote music for the Russian Orthodox church, an outstanding example being the *Liturgy of St. John Chrysostum,* and he died in 1943.

The English composer, **John Taverner** (1495–1545) had also collected examples of Greek Orthodox music, and made use of this tonality in his successful *Celtic Requiem*; Russian orchestras have maintained a distinctness of instrumentalisation, in which various sounds do not blend together as much as in orchestras of the West.

Peter Tchaikowsky's friend and confidant, **Madame Nadeghda von Meck,** travelled across Europe in 1879 with **Claude Achille Debussy,** the French composer, who was born in St. Germain-en-Laye in the year 1862. Debussy's early work was influenced by the German romantic operatic style of Richard Wagner, and in 1884 Debussy won the Prix de Rome with his cantata *L'Enfant prodige,* but then he branched off into a more experimental and individual style of composition with his first mature work, *L'Après-Midi d'un*

Faun, which was a prelude evoked by a poem by Mallarmé, and an operatic setting of Maeterlinck's *Pélleas et Melisand,* which he began in 1892, but which was not performed until 1902. Claude Debussy also wrote some outstanding piano pieces, "images" and "préludes," in which he moved further from traditional formulae and experimented with novel techniques and effects that produced the pictures in sound known as musical Impressionism. Debussy's orchestral piece *La Mer* is another example of musical Impressionism. He died in 1918.

The Revival of Interest in the Guitar

The guitar is not an instrument that can in any way be classified as an instrument of the orchestra, but after becoming known through folk music, it has gained popularity in a similar way to the saxophone through the attention devoted to this instrument by such well-known performers and composers of music for the guitar such as Julian Bream, John Williams and Andre Segovia.

The "Iberia Suite" by the Spanish composer **Frederico Albeniz** is reminiscent of the different regions of Spain which the composer encountered during his travels round this country, and the music also owes much to Claude Debussy's impressionistic style of composition.

The guitar concerto of **Joaquin Rodrigo** "Concierto de Aranjuez" was created by an inspiration similar to that of Ravel when he wrote "Boléro" for the orchestra, and indeed both composers were well acquainted with each other and were equally surprised at the success accorded to their compositions. Moreover, both composers can be identified by outstanding physical characteristics: Ravel was very small in stature, and Rodrigo, who was born in 1902, blind.

At the time when Rodrigo wrote the "Concierto de Aranjuez" the Spanish civil war had just drawn to a close, and the Spanish people were glad to hear music that reminded them of a bygone age when times were more settled and values more permanent, for the name "Aranjuez" is that of the magnificent summer residence of the Spanish king not far from Madrid, and the music incorporates the opulence of these associations with the flamboyance of the folk-lore tradition of the guitar, and in particular the "flamenco" style of playing the instrument with strumming effects. The conservative Spanish public welcomed back the old trusted form and style of composition and playing and Rodrigo was awarded richly for his success, which besides medals and official posts, included his appointment as professor of music at Madrid University.

Maurice Ravel (1875–1937) was also a student at the Paris Conservatory. He learnt the value of classical form from Gabriel Fauré (1845–1924) and was also influenced by Eric Satie (1866–1925), who opposed the heavy Wagnerian style of composition as being unsuited to the Latin temperament. Ravel's "Boléro" introduces African drum rhythms into the orchestra, as well as containing a remarkable saxophone solo at the beginning of the work.

The friendship of **Johannes Brahms** was a great influence and stimulus on the life of the young Czech composer, **Antonin Dvorak**. Brahms, who was born in Hamburg in 1833, used Eastern European folk melodies as a source of inspiration for many of his compositions, which included the *Hungarian Dances* and *Zigeuner Lider*. The *St. Anthony Choral*, which he composed on a theme of Joseph Haydn, remains one of his best loved works. In 1857 Brahms turned down the offer of an award of an honorary degree from the University of Cambridge, claiming that he was "too busy" to write a piece of music for the occasion.

Although Brahms toured widely within Germany giving performances of his compositions and playing the piano himself, which gained him the friendship of Robert and Clara Schumann, who were intrigued particularly by the "Handel Variations," which Brahms always performed himself, entirely from memory, on the piano. However, the same hostility was meted out to Brahms by the Viennese public as has greeted previous avant-garde composers such as Wolfgang Amadee Mozart and Franz Schubert.

In contrast, the German conductor, **Hans Guido von Bulow,** who was born in Dresden in 1834, and studied the piano with Franz Liszt, espoused the cause of Johannes Brahms and dropped the Wagnerians, although Brahms himself remained friends with that great exponent of the piano, Franz Liszt. Hans Guido von Bulow had married the daughter of Franz Liszt, Cosima, who later left him to marry Richard Wagner. Hans Guido von Bulow had the capacity, like Johannes Brahms, of conducting and playing entirely from memory, and on one occasion at Meinigen conducted a performance of the *Irish Symphony* by Charles Villiers Stanford without using a score himself and without any member of the orchestra having any music in front of him either.

Brahms loved to bring old German folk tunes into his music, and his ever-popular *Hungarian Rhapsodies* takes this development a stage further, introducing varied dance rhythms and new melodies into the music. Brahms himself was an enthusiastic walker, and on one occasion walked from Göttingen, where he had been holding a concert of his music, to Düsseldorf, a distance of some three hundred kilometres.

In 1879, the University of Breslau made Brahms a Doctor of Philosophy, giving him precedence over all other living composers of church music, especially in recognition of his great *German Requiem.* Brahms treated this university better than he had treated Cambridge University, for, at a concert given in honour of the event of conferring the degree, Brahms brought out two new compositions; the first of which had a evidently been written for the occasion, the "Academic Festival" overture. It is built upon student songs and winds up with "Gaudeamus," and was received with hearty enthusiasm. This overture was performed in England—at the Crystal Palace—under Manns, and shortly thereafter in concerts conducted by Carl Ricther. Brahms's "Tragic Overture" is marked by deep earnestness, resignation, and melancholy. Brahms died in 1897.

In 1873, **Antonin Dvorak,** who was born near Prague in 1841 and who began to earn his living by playing the viola in an orchestra in 1857, attracted attention for himself with the composition of "Hymnus," which is a nationalistic piece, based on Halek's poem "The Heroes of the White Mountain." Later, while organist at St. Adalbert's Church in Prague, Dvorak made a name for himself with several compositions that were promising enough to bring him to the notice of the authorities, and to secure him a state grant. In 1877 Brahms became a member of the committee that examined the compositions of state grant holders, and when he recognised Dvorak's talent, Brahms introduced the music of his protégé to the Viennese public by sponsoring Dvorak's *Klänge aus Mähren,* which was followed by the *Slavonic Dances.*

Dvorak's music won increasing acclaim, culminating in European acclaim for his *Sabat Mater,* which was first performed in London in 1883. By this time Dvorak had written six symphonies, as well as chamber and piano music, and the world-wide fame that he enjoyed eventually brought him, in 1891, the offer to become Director of the New York Conservatory. It was in America that Dvorak wrote the popular Ninth Symphony *From the New World,* which contains melodies reminiscent of American folk music, whilst retaining a distinct Slavonic flavour.

Sir Edward Elgar, who was born in 1857, was the last figure of outstanding genius produced by the English Renaissance. Edward Elgar was born in Broadheath, near Worcester, and he grew up within sight of the beautiful Black Mountains on the border of Wales. The house where Elgar was born is now a museum, which is open to the public, but it still exudes an atmosphere of peace and tranquillity. Elgar's father was organist at the local church, and a music dealer, but apart from lessons on playing the violin, the young Edward received no special musical education and taught himself the art of composition.

The *Enigma Variations,* which Elgar wrote in 1889, consolidated his reputation as Britain's leading figure in music, both at home and abroad, and his oratorio *The Dream of Gerontious,* written in the year 1900, further confirmed this position. The attraction of the *Engima Variations* lies in the nature of the puzzles or riddles, which Elgar asks his audience to solve. The first puzzle remains unsolved to this day: namely the origin of the theme of the "andante" in G minor upon which the variations are based. It was, we are told, already a well-known melody.

The second part of the puzzle is less difficult, as each of the fourteen variations that follow are a musical characterisation of the initials, Christian names, or nicknames of friends of the composer, all well-known personalities. The penultimate variation is dedicated to Lady Mary Trefusis, who at the time of composition was making a voyage by sea, and the passage played on the clarinet brings to mind the overture by Felix Mendelssohn entitled "Calm Seas and a Happy Journey." For the final variation, Elgar composed a self-portrait with the letters E, D, and U, as Edu was Edward Elgar's nickname.

Edward Elgar was knighted after the Elgar Festival in 1904, and was appointed "Master of the King's Musick" from 1924 onwards. His further works were two oratorios, *The Apostles* and *The Kingdom,* two symphonies, a violin concerto, and a concerto for violoncello, the rendering of which has been immortalised by a performance with cellist Jacqueline Du Pres, and conducted by Daniel Barenboim.

During the last night of the "Proms," which takes place in the Royal Albert Hall, London, at the end of the summer, the orchestra is accustomed to play Elgar's March 2, "Pomp and Circumstance." The audience invariably joins in with the words of the patriotic song "Land of Hope and Glory." This moving occasion can be watched by viewers of television all over the world, by virtue of satellite transmission.

Xylophones

The xylophone is essentially a very primitive instrument. The name comes from the Greek word *xylon,* meaning wood, which was the original material used for the blocks. They were first tuned and then laid across a cradle, or resonator. The blocks were nailed down at one end only, to improve the sonority when struck. Once the wooden blocks were replaced with metal ones, the xylophone really became a metallophone, and this in turn produced the instrument known as the celeste, which has been used with considerable effect by Tchaikowsky in his *Nutcracker Suite*.

The marimba of southern Mexico is one of the more popular and sophisticated members of the xylophone family, and often makes an appearance in Western music, although the most advanced version of this instrument is found in Southeast Asia.

A nonmelodic percussion instrument, the triangle, has been used in a delightful way to heighten the effect of orchestration, as in Beethoven's *Ninth Symphony,* the "Choral," and Johannes Brahms uses the instrument with subtle effect in his orchestration.

In **Hector Berlioz's** *Symphony Fantastique,* chimes can be heard in the section titled "Witches Sabbath." Berlioz makes use in his music of the saxophone, an instrument that has been neglected by subsequent composers, as it did not appear to warrant a permanent place in the orchestra. However, as a solo instrument, the saxophone has had more success. It was devised in Belgium by Adolf Sax in 1844, primarily to be played in military bands.

The French composer **Henri Tomas,** born in Marseilles in 1901, wrote a memorable passage for the saxophone in his music for the overture "Hamlet," and the instrument can be compared in tonal qualities to the clarinet, which is also a wind instrument requiring a single reed to produce the sound, whereas the oboe family and the bassoon require a double reed.

Hector Berlioz (1803–69) had a triumphant reception in Germany when he visited the country in the years 1852–57. In his overture "Harold in Italy" Berlioz portrays French romanticism in a musical characterisation of some of its more sinister and grotesque aspects, as in the scene of the brigands dancing round their campfire.

In 1993 a manuscript as found in an organ-loft in the city of Antwerp which contained a hitherto unknown mass composed by Hector Berlioz. His music had previously been considered as the musical expression of his literary ideas.

Cymbals have also gradually found their way into

orchestral music, for perhaps surprisingly, the realm of the nonmelodic percussion instruments is one where the highly sophisticated modern symphony orchestra most readily meets the long traditions of folk and ethnic music. Nevertheless, in an age when the mainstream of Western classical music is in considerable disarray, the continuing existence of living folk traditions, such as those of Central and South America, with their very distinctive rhythms and timbres, provides a refreshing and hopeful source of pleasure and inspiration, as well as proof of enormous resilience to external pressures, in a world that is all too prone to exploit ethnic diversity for its own ends.

George Bizet (1838–75) calls for the use of cymbals to great effect in his opera *Carmen*, which is nowadays regarded as the most popular opera ever to have been written—rivalled only perhaps by the modern musicals produced by Lord Lloyd-Weber, such as *Sunset Boulevard*.

Hungarian composer **Bela Bartok** was born in Nagyszentmiklos in 1881 and began his own musical education as soon as he was able to hold his hands on the keyboard. His first lessons were given to him by his mother. Bartok's relationship to music grew to fill every need of childhood, which was spent in complete isolation, due to a skin complaint that made him reluctant to see anyone outside the family. Bartok's father died when his son was seven years old, and his mother was left with responsibility of furthering her son's musical education. After long years of continuous moving, the family with two children eventually settled in the city of Pozsony, which provided the cultural atmosphere they were looking for.

Bartok entered the Budapest Academy of Music at the suggestion of the Hungarian composer Dohnanyi, who lived from 1877 until 1960. After studying under Istvan Thoman, who had been a pupil of Franz Liszt, Bartok thereafter toured widely as a pianist. At first Bartok's own compositions were influenced by the music of Liszt and Wagner, and later by those of Richard Strauss and Claude Debussy, but his deepest and most lasting inspiration was drawn from Hungarian peasant songs. Bartok's collection of folk songs, which he started in 1905, forms a treasury of national music quite different from the popular and gypsy music used by earlier Hungarian composers, and different again from the melodies used by Johannes Brahms in his Hungarian compositions.

He was appointed as professor at Bratislava University, later part of Czechoslovakia. Ultimately, Bartok's antifascist views rendered it impossible for him to remain in the country, and after the death of his mother in 1939, he immigrated to America, where he was able to work on the classification of Yugoslav music held by Harvard University and on his collection of Romanian melodies. He died in 1945.

When Bela Bartok first arrived in the United States of America, he always performed the concertos on the piano playing with the music in front of him, which gave an impression of amateurism, but actually the pianist Clara Schumann, wife of Robert Schumann, never played from memory when performing in a concert.

Györgi Sandor Ligeti is a modern Hungarian composer, born in 1923. Like Bartok, he studied at the Budapest Academy of Music, where he later taught. Ligeti also researched into Hungarian folk music, and he wrote some folk-song arrangements.

It was not until he left Hungary in 1956 that Ligeti became seriously interested in composition: he worked in Germany for a time and produced "Articulation for Tape" at the electronics studio in Cologne in 1958, but thereafter worked only with live performers. His name became widely known through "Apparitions," which was written in the year 1958–59. In "Atmospheres," which followed in 1969, Ligeti demonstrates his technique of chromatic complexes, and in "Aventures," written in 1962, and "Nouvelles Aventures," 1962–65, he used his own invented language of speech sounds.

Ligeti's wind quintet, while making the conventional use of wind instruments, produces a characteristic, but convincing combination of tone colour and rhythmic effects.

Györgi Ligeti has held academic posts in Stockholm, California, and Hamburg, and is a member of the Hamburg Free Academy of Arts and the Royal Academy of Arts recently he has been voicing his protest at the irresponsible and "barbaric" attempt to close down the International Institute for Traditional Music in Berlin. The Music Institute has been leading in the field of music and ethnology, and is the only one that uses German as the first language. Only London, Paris, and Washington have comparable institutions. Ligeti claims that, since 1991, six hundred million marks have been struck from Berlin's cultural budget, deletions having included the closure of Berlin's main theatre, the Schiller Theatre.

Jazz

Leonard Bernstein, who was born in 1903 and died in 1990, wrote *West Side Story* in 1958, creating a musical event that fused both European and American traditions, in a plot based on Shakespeare's *Romeo and Juliet,* including two rival families, with the introduction of the colour and ethnic element as a further distinguishing feature of the two groups, "Jets" and "Sharks."

George Gershwin, who was born in New York in 1898, studied music in the traditional way, but he wrote his first song when he was fourteen years of age, and later became famous as a writer of Broadway musicals. George collaborated with his brother, Ira, to produce *Lady Be Good,* which they wrote together in 1924, which was followed by *Of Thee I Sing* in 1931. Gershwin was commissioned by Paul Whiteman to write *Rhapsody in Blue,* which embodies both romantic emotionalism with the jazz idiom. The opening "glissando" passage on the clarinet achieves an usual effect, as well as a display of virtuosity on the part of the performer. George and Ira's black opera, *Porgy and Bess* from the year 1935, won international popularity, still runs as a box office success, and brought a combination of skill and sincerity not only to symphonic jazz, but also to the modern song.

Benjamin David "Benny" Goodman was born in 1909 in a Chicago ghetto, the last of twelve children of an immigrant tailor who had fled from Russian anti-Semitism. Benny received his first clarinet and other musical training from a local synagogue. Benny continued his studies through "Hull House," a social service agency for the under-privileged. His most important teacher was Franz Schoeppe, who as a classical instructor from the Chicago Musical College disdained jazz, and instilled in his students respect for classical musicianship.

After his father died, the fourteen-year-old Benny helped to support his family by playing at a Chicago neighbourhood dance hall, where he worked for two years. In 1925, Goodman was hired by band leader and drummer Ben Pollack, and between "gigs," Benny performed with members of the Austin High Gang, who introduced him to the New Orleans Rhythm Kings, and the "Dixieland" clarinet style of Leon Rappolo.

In 1933, Goodman accepted an offer by the legendary producer John Hammond, to record for Columbia's English market, which was more receptive to jazz than were the Americans. In that year also, Benny appeared at the last recording session of Bessie Smith, and the first of Billie Holiday. Hammond urged Benny Goodman to hire Teddy Wilson and Lionel Hampton for his small combo, which also included drummer Gene Krupa. In this way the group became the first interracial jazz ensemble to perform in public. Benny Goodman lived until 1986.

Alfred Schnitke was born in 1934 in Engels, near Saratov, into a Russian-Jewish family. His musical studies began in 1946 in Vienna, where his father worked for a Soviet-German language newspaper. In 1948 Alfred Schnitke moved to Moscow, trained as a choir master, and from 1953–58 studied composition at Moscow Music Conservatory, where he later taught from 1962 to 1972.

The prolific output of Alfred Schnitke has attracted more attention from critics in the West than any Soviet composer since Dmitri Shostakovich, and it is characterised by bold eclectic flair and frequent reference to music of the past together with popular influences such as the jazz idiom. Underlying Alfred Schnitke's originality and experimental tendencies his music has retained the formal melodic and harmonic characteristics that anchor him in the mainstream of Russian music, and now at sixty years of age, Schnitke has succeeded Györgi Ligeti at his post in Hamburg.

The Russian composer **Dmitri Shostakovich** was born in St. Petersburg in 1906, and in 1919 he entered the St. Petersburg Music Conservatory. In 1925 Shostakovich composed his *First Symphony,* in which he attempted to support Soviet principles, and he attracted considerable attention for himself and his music. However, with the development of a more conservative attitude on the part of the Soviet government, which coincided with a more experimental outlook on the part of Shostakovich, official criticism was levelled at his opera *The Nose,* which was based on Gogol's story of the same name, written in 1836. A second opera, *A Lady Macbeth of Mtsensk,* had to be withdrawn after violent press attacks on its decadence and its failure to observe the principles of "Soviet realism." The *Second (October) Symphony* of Shostakovich was deemed unworthy of performance for similar reasons, but Shostakovich was reinstated after official approval of his *Fifth Symphony,* which he composed in 1938.

A similar fate befell the Russian composer and pianist **Sergei Sergeyevich Prokofiev,** who was born in the Ukraine in 1891. After studying at the Moscow Conservatory, he left Russia after the October Revolution to spend the next eighteen years in America. After he returned to Moscow in 1936, Prokofiev was able to write music for the films of the Russian film *regisseur* Sergei Eisenstein, such as *Potemkin.* After his health declined, however, first at the outbreak of the Second World War, and later when his wife was sent to a labour camp in 1948, Prokofiev was named by the Communist Party Central Committee as the composer of music "marked with formalist perversions ... alien to the Soviet people." Besides his *First Symphony,* the "Classical," Prokofiev is best known in the West for his chamber music, and especially by children of all ages, for the story with orchestral accompaniment "Peter and the Wolf," in which the bird fluttering in the branches of the tree is portrayed by the flute, the duck swimming on the pond by the oboe, the part of the grandfather is played by the bassoon, and the horn is sounded when the hunters ride into view. The tune of the cat is played on the clarinet.

Giuseppe Verdi (1813–1901) was twenty-eight years of

age when he was finally successful with is opera *Nabucodonsor* as it was at first called. The chorus of the prisoners at the beginning of the work, *"va pensiero sull' ali dorate,"* has become a by-word for Italian nationalism; this may have been only a subconscious wish of Verdi's, as the words had been used before in a ballet of the same name by Niccolo Cortesi.

The libretto had been written by Temisocle Solera who lived from 1815 until 1878, for Otto Nicolai, who had however turned it down. Verdi's opera was so successful that it was performed no less than seventy-five times in 1842 at the opera house La Scala in Milan. This was followed in 1844 by performances in Berlin, Stuttgart, and Korfu, where the name was abbreviated to *Nabucco,* which was to be final one.

Benjamin Britten, later to become Baron Britten of Aldeburgh, was born in Lowestoft in 1913. He won a scholarship to the Royal College of Music, after he had studied the piano with Harold Samuel, and composition with Frank Bridge, and worked under John Ireland. During the 1930s, Britten wrote the choral variations, *A Boy Is Born* and wrote music for films and commentaries; he also collaborated with W. H. Auden who provided the text for the song cycle *Our Hunting Fathers,* which anticipates and commiserates with potential victims over the fate which was threatening the German Jews. Due to health reasons, Britten was allowed to spend the war years in America, where he wrote a violin concerto, which explores new techniques and styles of virtuosity on the instrument, and the *Symphonia da Requiem.*

On his return to Britain, Benjamin Britten composed the *Variations and Fugue on a Theme of Purcell,* which is subtitled "The Young Person's Guide to the Orchestra," as each instrument is dealt with individually. Britten also wrote a cello concerto and music for the Russian cellist, Rostropovich, and music for the viola for Cecil Aronowitz. Britten set to music poems by the Russian poet Alexander Pushkin, and wrote a work for tenor horn and choir for his life-long friend Peter Pears. "Gloriana" was written for the coronation of Queen Elizabeth II in 1952. The Britten opera *A Midsummer Night's Dream* is based on William Shakespeare's play, which had also inspired Henry Purcell to write a musical drama. Because Benjamin Britten wrote music of a national character, he has been called the Verdi of Britain.

Benjamin Britten's *Nebuchandnezzar,* the title role of which he wrote for Peter Pears, deals with the subject of isolation and alienation in a strange land, represented by the Israelites in Babylon, where they were misunderstood and oppressed. In the ancient biblical text, a sackbut is the musical instrument that is mentioned, and the music for this part is written for the trombone: in the percussion section in which recording the drummer James Blades brings forth a spring taken from a railway train to produce the abrasive sound that was required in the music.

Britten also set poems by Walter de la Mare and Christina Rossetti to music, as well as the *Songs and Proverbs of William Blake,* which were performed at Aldeburgh in 1965 by Dietrich Fischer-Dieskau. These were seen by the critics as Britten's deepest and most subtle expression through the music of the darkness and cruelty that some of the words evoked, and as themes which haunted Britten's music. He died in 1976.

The Secret of Music

The attempts by scientists to explain the allure of

music and its effect on the nervous system and its working on the brain can only partially succeed; this has to do with an emotional response the functioning of which is still unknown, even to medical specialists. Music in this sense, therefore, can be called medicine for the soul, enabling or indeed forcing the listener to distinguish between what is the same from that which is different; only music that does not vary in tone or intensity can be said to have a deadening effect on its audience.

The fact that music that is popular and economically successful at one time does not necessarily have permanent value for future generations is illustrated by the esteemed status of Antonio Salieri in Vienna, at a time when Wolfgang Amadee Mozart, and indeed Salieri's own pupil, Franz Schubert were struggling for a living. Wolfgang Amadee Mozart's youngest surviving son, Franz Xavier, took lessons from Antonio Salieri, and his *Second Piano Concerto,* which dates from 1814, was deemed to be a success, due to the fact that it exactly tailored to meet the demands of the prevailing taste in music.

When a composer writes a piece of music such as an oratorio, it can also reflect the spiritual and political problems of the times, as does **Sir Michael Tippet**'s great work *A Child of Our Time,* which was written in 1941. Sir Michael was imprisoned for three months during World War II because of his conscientious objection to miliary service. Michael Tippett (b. 1905) was created CBE in 1959 and he received his knighthood in 1966.

Conclusion

While a single instrument can pick out a theme or tune in a musical score, only the full orchestra playing in concert can fill out the whole picture in the same way in which a skilled artist can present us with a finished portrait. Whether or not the orchestra itself can be viewed as a single instrument is open to debate; however it takes an experienced conductor to gain control of the modern orchestra so that it can give expression to the conductor's own rendering of a particular composition. In previous centuries the composer would have conducted his own work from the harpsichord, and would certainly have conducted the first performance of his composition, or played the part of the soloist as did Mozart and Beethoven in their piano concertos. This is done in the present day only when an attempt is being made to recreate the conditions under which the music would have been performed in the past, and to play a work such as Beethoven's *Ninth Symphony* involving a full-scale choir would be almost unthinkable. In his final chorus, "Ode to Joy," Beethoven calls upon his listeners to seek for those qualities which act to unite, rather than divide mankind.*

The American singer, **Elvis Presley,** who was "discovered" in 1954 after he had privately made a gramophone record for his mother, was a pioneer in his ability to com-

---

*Based on the poem by Freidrick Schiller.

bine "country" singing and guitar playing with African rhythms and melodies, an art form which the American singer Diana Reeves has also mastered to become a way of life.

The theme of immortality is captured in a few lines by the British poet John Keats in his poem "Ode to the Nightingale," which he wrote in 1819:

> Thou wast not born for death immortal bird!
> No hungry generations tread thee down;
> The voice I hear this passing night was heard
> In ancient days by emperor and clown

Finally, the personality of the musician, whether conductor or performer, directly affects the interpretation of a composer's work; the same piece of music may sound completely different when performed by contrasting artists with a different emotional response to the composition.

Leibnitz, the German philosopher and mathematician who formulated the system of calculus before Sir Isaac Newton, maintains that mankind must seek for harmony with himself and with nature.

The contemporary composer **Barbara Heller** has composed a piece titled "Emergency," dealing with the subject of a fire which breaks out after a car crash in which the occupants are killed. Music from Bach's *St. Matthew Passion* contrasts with insertions of modern tonal progressions depicting agitation, grief, and despair. The music is accompanied by a reading describing the action which has taken place, and the performance has a cohesion as a lament for tragedies past and present.

References

Beethoven; His Life and Work. Hamlyn Publishing Group, 1990.
Carpenter, Humphrey. *Benjamin Britten; a Biography.* London: Faber and Faber, 1992.
"Culture in the Court of Henry VIII," *History Today,* vol. 41. Dowling, June 1993.
Dean, Roger T. *New Structures in Jazz and Improvised Music since 1960.* Open University Press, n.d.
Dictionary of Music. 1958.
Erb, J. Lawrence. *Brahms.* J. Dent & Sons Ltd., 1925.
Fasset, Agatha. *The Naked Face of Genius: Bela Bartok's Last Years.* London: Lowe and Brydone, 1958.
Hogwood, Christopher. *George Frederick Handel.* London: Thames and Hudson, 1984.
Hopkins, Anthony. *Sounds of Music.* Guildford, London, Oxford, and Worcester: for J. Dent and Sons by Billing and Sons, 1982.
Johann Sebastian Bach, His Life and Work. Hamlyn Publishing Group, 1990.
Kendall, Alan. *Musical Instruments.* Hamlyn Publishing Group, 1972.
King, Robert. *Henry Purcell.* Thomas & Hudson, 1994.
Landon, H. C. Robbins. *Mozart's Last Year, 1791.* Flamingo, 1990.
Leopold, Silke. *Monteverdi: Music in Transition.* Oxford: Clarendon Press, 1991.
Oberman, Heiko A. *Luther; Man between God and the Devil.* Fontana Press, 1993.
Ostow, Robin. *Jews in Contemporary East Germany: The Children of Moses in the Land of Marx.* London: Maximillian Press, 1989.
Parry, J. R. *A Protestant Vision: William Harrison and the Reforma-

tion of Elizabethan England. Cambridge: Cambridge University Press, 1987.
The Reader's Encyclopaedia, 3rd Edition, William Rose Benet, ed., 1977.
The Secret Warfare of Freemasonry against Church and State. Translated from the German. London: Burns & Oats, 1875.
Short, Michael. Gustav Holst, the Man and His Music. Oxford: Oxford University Press, 1990.
Stroh'm, Reinhard. Music in Late Medieval Bruges. Oxford: Clarendon Paperbacks, 1992.
Tchaikowsky, His Life and Work. Hamlyn Publishing Group, 1990.
Till, Nicholas. Mozart and the Enlightenment. London: Faber and Faber, 1992.